DATE DUE

JUN - 5 2013		
MAY 1 8 2015		
JUL - 2 2015		
JAN 3 0 2016		
SEP 0 4 2018		
JUL 1 0 2019		

DEMCO 38-296

ARIZONA

Past and Present

Corona Brezina

rosen publishing's
rosen central

New York

Published in 2010 by The Rosen Publishing Group, Inc.
29 East 21st Street, New York, NY 10010

First Edition

Library of Congress Cataloging-in-Publication Data

Brezina, Corona.
Arizona: past and present / Corona Brezina.
   p. cm.—(The United States: past and present)
Includes bibliographical references and index.
ISBN 978-1-4358-3516-0 (library binding)
ISBN 978-1-4358-8483-0 (pbk)
ISBN 978-1-4358-8482-3 (6 pack)
1. Arizona—Juvenile literature. I. Title.
F811.3.B74 2010
979.1—dc22

2009017004

Manufactured in the United States of America

CPSIA Compliance Information: Batch #LW10YA: For Further Information contact Rosen Publishing, New York, New York at 1-800-237-9932

On the cover: Top left: The ruins of the O.K. Corral in Tombstone, Arizona. Top right: The Arizona farming industry. Bottom: The Grand Canyon.

Contents

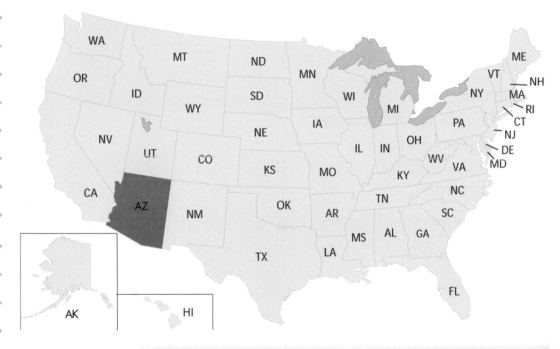

Though Arizona's beauty awes visitors, the hot summer temperatures can be daunting. The state is sparsely populated; most residents live in the metropolitan areas of Phoenix and Tucson.

Introduction

Mention "Arizona" and people immediately see images of saguaro cacti, vast deserts, and the Grand Canyon. Tourists visit Arizona to see many natural wonders in addition to the Grand Canyon. These wonders have evocative names like the Painted Desert, Petrified Forest, Canyon de Chelly, Superstition Mountains, Sunset Crater Volcano, Seven Falls Trail, and Window Rock. The state is also known for its sunny weather, Wild West legacy, and rich Native American heritage—it has the most Indian territory of all the states.

Although famous for its desert landscape, Arizona is also mountainous. There are even majestic forests in some areas of the state. Arizona has a number of large lakes that were created when rivers were dammed. There are ghost towns, ancient Native American ruins, and guest ranches. But people also flock to the golf courses, resorts, and cultural attractions there. Late in his life, renowned architect Frank Lloyd Wright built Taliesin West in central Arizona as a winter school of architecture.

Long before Arizona was part of the United States, Native Americans farmed it. It was the Indians who were the first people to irrigate the land and grow crops. Later on came the Spanish conquistadors, missionaries, ranchers, trappers, miners, and settlers. Arizona was claimed by Spain and then Mexico. Finally, the United States gained possession of Arizona through treaty and land purchase. This began the era of the Wild West that people most associate with Arizona—a frontier land of outlaws and sheriffs, ranchers and prospectors, cattle rustlers, bandits, cowboys, gamblers, and Native American warriors. Arizona's Wild West days drew to a law-abiding close by the time it officially became a state in 1912.

Today, Arizona relies more on tourism, high-tech industries, and manufacturing than mining and ranching. Shootouts in saloons only occur in historical reenactments. The state's population surged in the second half of the twentieth century. Arizona faces challenges, such as ongoing water issues, economic troubles, and debate over illegal immigration. But both Arizonans and visitors alike will continue to fall in love with the state with the endless sunny skies.

Chapter 1

THE GEOGRAPHY OF ARIZONA

With an area of 114,007 square miles (295,278 square kilometers), Arizona is the sixth-largest state in the United States. It is located in the western region of the country and is bordered by Utah to the north, Nevada and California to the west, Mexico to the south, and New Mexico to the east. Arizona is known as one of the "Four Corners" states because at its northeast corner, Utah, Colorado, Arizona, and New Mexico meet at a crossroads. Arizona's largest cities are Phoenix, which is the state capital, and Tucson.

Geographic Features

Northern Arizona is part of the Colorado Plateau, an elevated land-mass that extends into parts of Utah, Colorado, and New Mexico. With average elevations between 5,000 and 8,000 feet (1,524 and 2,438 meters), the Colorado Plateau features mountains, striking rock formations, and thousands of canyons whittled by rivers and streams. The most famous of these canyons is the Grand Canyon, which is considered to be one of the Seven Wonders of the World. Arizona's highest point is Humphrey's Peak, at 12,633 feet (3,851 m). It rises from the San Francisco Peaks, a range of mountains near Flagstaff on the Colorado Plateau. Also near Flagstaff is Meteor

Crater, a well-preserved crater about 4,000 feet (1,200 m) across—about the area of twenty football fields—that was created by an impact about fifty thousand years ago.

The southern boundary of the Colorado Plateau is the Mogollon Rim, a stretch of sheer cliffs that extends for about 300 miles (482 km) from the middle of the state to the southeast. South of the Colorado Plateau is the Central Mountain region, or the Transition Zone. This narrow region consists of steep chains of mountains. Many of Arizona's mountains are the remnants of volcanic activity, and hundreds of craters still exist.

The Colorado River snakes through the Grand Canyon. The cliffs reveal layers of limestone, sandstone, and shale from periods of the earth's history.

Most of southern Arizona is part of a geographic region of the Southwest called the Basin and Range. There, valleys and flat plains separate mountain ranges. Since the nineteenth century, treasure hunters searching for gold have flocked to one of these ranges, the Superstition Mountains, in search of the legendary Lost Dutchman

Mine. In the southwest corner of the state, the elevations are lower and give way to wide expanses of desert.

The major river in Arizona is the Colorado River, which flows through the Grand Canyon. It enters from Utah, meanders to the west, forms most of the state's western border, and continues into Mexico. Many of Arizona's rivers and streambeds are dry for much of the year, but torrential rains can fill them and cause flash floods.

Arizona's largest lakes are man-made, created by damming rivers. These include Lake Powell, which Arizona shares with Utah; Lake Mead and Lake Mojave, which are both shared with Nevada; and Lake Havasu, which is shared with California. Theodore Roosevelt Lake is located in central Arizona.

Deserts of Arizona

Nearly two-thirds of Arizona's land is desert. Arizona actually consists of four different deserts, each with a distinct climate. The Great Basin desert, in the northern section of the state, covers part of the Colorado Plateau. It is the coldest of the state's deserts and supports little vegetation other than shrubs, such as sagebrush. The portion of the Great Basin Desert in northeast Arizona is called the Painted Desert. To the northwest is the Mojave Desert, which is the driest of the state's deserts. It can be cold in the winter and blisteringly hot in the summer. The southeastern corner of Arizona extends into the Chihuahuan Desert.

To the southwest is the Sonoran Desert, which covers about a third of the state. It is the most beautiful and is rich in biodiversity. It is the warmest desert and receives the most rainfall of any in the United States. More than three-quarters of Arizona's population lives in the Sonoran Desert.

Few plants can survive in the Mojave Desert of northwestern Arizona, which receives less than 5 inches (12.7 cm) of rain annually. The Mojave has hot summers and frigid winters.

Parkland and Reservations

Only about 15 percent of Arizona's land is privately owned. Nearly 60 percent of state land is managed or owned by the federal or state government. This includes many forests, parks, and national monuments that are open to the public.

Arizona's most famous park is the Grand Canyon National Park. But the state possesses many other spectacular sites of natural beauty. At the Petrified Forest National Park in the Painted Desert, visitors can see a plain of fallen trees that were transformed into colorful stone, as well as ancient petroglyphs left by prehistoric Pueblo people and exhibits of fossils. Monument Valley, in northeast Arizona, features dramatic mesas, buttes, and other sandstone rock formations. Saguaro National Park, near Tucson, showcases the saguaro cactus, as well as an abundant variety of desert wildlife.

Twenty-three Native American tribes own slightly more than 25 percent of Arizona's land. The Navajo Nation possesses the largest reservation, with an area of 25,351 square miles (65,658 sq km), in the United States. The largest portion of the reservation is in northeastern Arizona. The Hualapai, Havasupai, Apache, Tohono O'odham, Gila River Indians, and Colorado River Indians also hold significant areas of land in their reservations.

Climate

Most Arizonans enjoy clear skies and low humidity. But the southern region of Arizona experiences scorching heat in the summer. Average daily temperatures in Phoenix exceed 100 degrees Fahrenheit (38 degrees Celsius) during the summer months. Average winter temperatures are around 60°F (16°C), although nighttime temperatures can drop below freezing. Since temperatures fall as the altitude rises, the Colorado Plateau and mountainous areas are cooler.

Rainfall patterns generally correlate with elevation—the southern desert typically receives less than 5 inches (13 centimeters) of rain annually, while the mountains and Colorado Plateau can receive more than 25 inches (64 cm). Much of Arizona experiences violent thunderstorms in the late summer. In high-altitude areas, winter storms can bring significant snowfall.

The Grand Canyon

Located in northern Arizona, the Grand Canyon extends for 277 miles (445.7 km) and, on average, is 10 miles (16 km) wide and 1 mile (1.6 km) deep. The Grand Canyon was formed over a period of time beginning five to ten million years ago. As the Colorado Plateau rose upward, the Colorado River began to carve down through the layers of rock. Since each stratum of rock dates from a different period in Earth's geological record, fossils from the Grand Canyon offer valuable insight about the evolution of life over the eons.

Native Americans have inhabited the Grand Canyon on and off for ten thousand years. In 1869, John Wesley Powell led the first American expedition through the Grand Canyon.

Tourism at the Grand Canyon began to thrive with the arrival of the railroad in 1901. President Theodore Roosevelt visited the Grand Canyon in 1903, and it was designated a national monument in 1908. It officially became a national park in 1919.

Today, the Grand Canyon National Park encompasses 1,904 square miles (4,931 sq km). It's a symbol of the grandeur of the Southwest that is visited by five million people every year. Visitors can explore the canyon itself, as well as nearby waterfalls, Indian reservations, rock formations, and other sights.

John Wesley Powell—an anthropologist, geologist, and explorer who lost an arm in the Civil War—published a riveting and widely read account of his Grand Canyon expedition.

A saguaro cactus towers above Arizona's Painted Desert. The pleats in the trunk can expand to allow for rapid absorption of water, and a full-grown saguaro weighs more than 6 tons.

The Wildlife of Arizona

Each geographic and climatic region of Arizona supports a different assortment of plants and animals. The Sonoran Desert is famous for the saguaro cactus, which can reach a height of 50 feet (15 m) and live for 150 years. Woodpeckers peck holes and nest inside the cacti. Other desert birds, such as wrens and owls, move into the abandoned holes in the stem. Additional wildlife of the Sonoran includes jackrabbits, coyotes, whiptail lizards, roadrunners, kangaroo rats, rattlesnakes, poisonous Gila monsters, horned toads, scorpions, tortoises, and mountain lions. Jaguars sometimes venture into Arizona from Mexico. There are also flowering plants; many different cacti, including the cholla cactus; and various small shrubs and trees like Joshua trees and thick groves of mesquite, a small spiny tree. Pronghorns and bighorn sheep graze at slightly higher elevations in the Sonoran Desert.

At higher altitudes, the desert gives way to woodlands and forests. The largest ponderosa pine forest in the United States grows in the northern part of Arizona. Above elevations of 7,500 feet (2,286 m), the landscape is similar to that of Canada. Dense forests of firs and pines provide habitat for deer, elk, black bears, wild turkeys, bobcats, and mountain lions. Arizona's mountain ecosystems are sometimes referred to as "sky islands," since creatures that thrive at higher elevations could never move across the desert to another mountain "island." They support a rich diversity of wildlife, some of it unique to the sky island ecosystem.

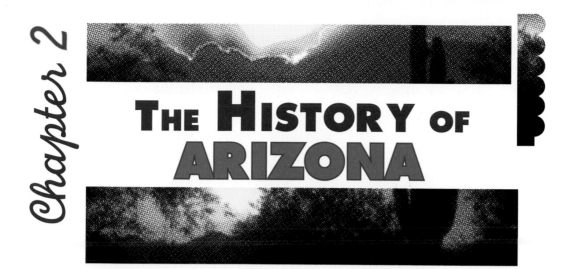

THE HISTORY OF ARIZONA

Arizona's history begins long before the arrival of the Spanish, Mexicans, or white Americans. The first Native Americans arrived about fifteen thousand years ago, and survived by hunting and gathering. Around 2,000 BCE, they began cultivating crops, and their nomadic way of life gradually gave way to fixed communities. By 700 CE, three distinct cultures had developed. The Hohokam farmed in the central and southern deserts, and the Mogollon lived in the highlands to the east. The Ancestral Puebloans, also called the Anasazi, occupied the northern plateau, where they constructed elaborate cliff dwellings in canyons. All three cultures abandoned their homelands between 1300 and 1450, possibly because of drought.

Such groups as the Pueblo people (including the Hopi), Pima, and Tohono O'odham are thought to be descendents of the three ancient tribes. Between 1300 and 1600, the Navajo and Apache migrated southward from Canada and Alaska. They led a nomadic existence of hunting and gathering.

Exploration and Settlement

The first European to explore Arizona was a Spanish Franciscan priest named Marcos de Niza. He led a 1539 expedition in search of

The San Xavier del Bac Mission, built on the site founded by Father Eusebio Kino, is one of the finest examples of Spanish colonial architecture in the United States.

the legendary Seven Cities of the Cíbola, supposedly the source of great treasure. The conquistador Francisco Vàsquez de Coronado followed in 1540, leading 336 soldiers and nearly 1,000 Native American allies. He explored the Southwest for two years. Coronado found no gold but began a pattern of strife between Europeans and Pueblo natives.

In 1598, Juan de Oñate founded the colony of New Mexico, which extended across most of the Southwest. He established a settlement near present-day Santa Fe. Ranchers seized huge tracts of land in the new colony, and priests set up missions so that they could convert the Native Americans to Christianity. In 1680, a Pueblo uprising drove the Spanish out of New Mexico.

Farther to the south, a Jesuit priest named Father Eusebio Kino began establishing Christian missions in 1691. In addition to his missionary work, he introduced new agricultural methods and livestock.

The Spanish continued to extend their presence in Arizona, despite occasional conflicts with Native Americans. The first Spanish settlement was established in 1752 near present-day Tucson, and settlers, ranchers, farmers, and miners began moving northward. The Mexican War of Independence began in 1810, but the fighting did not reach Arizona. In 1821, the Spanish recognized Mexico's independence, and Arizona became part of the newly established Republic of Mexico.

The Wild West

The first non-Spanish Europeans to settle in Arizona were fur trappers and traders who arrived in the early nineteenth century. From 1846 to 1847, the United States and Mexico fought the Mexican-American War. The conflict did not extend to Arizona, but the Treaty of Guadalupe Hidalgo ceded the area from California across to Texas to the United States. Most of Arizona became part of the New Mexico Territory. The southern part of Arizona was added in 1854 through the Gadsden Purchase agreement with Mexico. The military began establishing forts across Arizona, and ranchers and farmers started moving in. During the Civil War (1861–1865), Arizona declared itself the Confederate Territory of Arizona (CSA). The Union recaptured the CSA in 1862.

The O.K. Corral

The most notorious shootout in the Old West took place on October 26, 1881, at the O.K. Corral in the southeastern Arizona town of Tombstone. Virgil Earp was city marshal of the rowdy frontier town, and he had appointed his brothers Morgan and Wyatt Earp, and their friend Doc Holliday, as deputies. Wyatt had a reputation for operating outside the law on occasion.

The Earp brothers had a strong rivalry with the county sheriff, John Behan, and two rancher clans, the Clantons and the McLowerys. In September, Virgil Earp ordered the arrest of one of Behan's deputies on the charge of robbing a stagecoach. Ike Clanton paid the man's bail.

In the prelude to the shootout, Ike Clanton exchanged insults with Doc Holliday, and Virgil Earp arrested Clanton for carrying firearms in town. The two sides met in a vacant lot outside the O.K. Corral: the Earps and Doc Holliday against two McLowerys and two Clantons. Gunfire erupted, and Billy Clanton, Frank McLowery, and Tom McLowery were killed. Virgil Earp, Morgan Earp, and Doc Holliday were wounded.

The Earps claimed that before firing, they called on their adversaries to give up their guns. Nobody knows for sure whether this is true or not. A judge found that their actions at O.K. Corral were justified.

Two months later, Virgil Earp was shot and wounded by gunmen. Three months after that, Morgan Earp was shot and killed. Wyatt Earp and Doc Holliday hunted down and killed two of the men that they blamed for Morgan Earp's death. One of them was Behan's deputy. After that, the pair fled Arizona.

Today, Tombstone is a national historic landmark, much of its Old West downtown preserved. O.K. Corral is a museum, and the Tombstone Courthouse is a state historic site. Tourists can watch reenactments of the famous gunfight. In addition, the O.K. Corral showdown has inspired numerous novels, historical accounts, and movies like *Tombstone* and *Wyatt Earp*.

In 1863, Congress officially established a separate territory of Arizona. In ongoing Indian Wars, the military fought to subdue the Native Americans, whom they viewed as a threat to settlements. In 1864, Kit Carson subdued and captured eight thousand Navajo by destroying their crops and livestock. They were sent on a grueling "Long Walk" of 370 miles (575 km), during which hundreds died, to remote Bosque Redondo in New Mexico. There, more than two thousand Native Americans died of smallpox and starvation. In 1868, they were allowed

Kit Carson was a soldier, explorer, and scout. Despite twice marrying native women, he drove the Navajo and Apache from their territory.

to return to a newly established Navajo reservation. Meanwhile, Chief Cochise, succeeded by Geronimo, led an Apache rebellion that ended when Geronimo surrendered in 1886.

Prospectors discovered that gold, silver, and copper were present in the region. After Arizona became a territory, more and more people arrived to seek their fortune in mining, ranching cattle and sheep, or farming near rivers and streams. Beginning in the 1870s, lawless mining boomtowns sprung up overnight when someone struck gold or silver. The Wild West gained a reputation as a place where laws were disregarded and disagreements were settled with guns.

Arizona's days as an untamed frontier drew to a close in the 1880s, when railroads were laid across the state. The city of Phoenix was incorporated in 1881. The U.S. Marshals and Arizona Rangers, which operated from 1901 to 1909, gradually brought order to the territory.

Statehood and Growth

In 1912, Arizona became the forty-eighth state in the United States. The new state's first governor was Democrat George W. P. Hunt, who had arrived in Arizona in 1881 as a penniless miner. Arizona prospered during World War I (1914–1918), when the price of copper was high. It suffered during the Great Depression (1929–1940). Then it rebounded upon the onset of World War II in 1941. The war effort required copper, cotton, and cattle, and the defense industries set up factories in Arizona. The Army Air Corps built bases in the state, taking advantage of the clear skies. One disgraceful chapter in U.S. history also took place in Arizona at this time. Many Japanese American citizens were confined to internment camps there because the U.S. government doubted their loyalty as Americans. German and Italian prisoners of war were also held in camps in Arizona.

Beginning in the twentieth century, Arizona began addressing its lack of water. A number of dams were built to provide a steady source of water to Arizona residents. The Theodore Roosevelt Dam was completed in 1911. The massive Hoover Dam, on the border with Nevada, was completed in 1936. The Central Arizona Project, a water diversion system from the Colorado River, was started in 1973 and reached Tucson in 1991.

When it was built, the Hoover Dam was the world's tallest. Today, it generates electricity and provides a steady water supply for residents of the Southwest.

After the introduction of air-conditioning in the 1950s, Arizona's population began to grow rapidly—a trend that continues today. Retirees and tourists make Arizona a destination. A large Native American population, the third largest in the nation, and a large Hispanic population contribute to the state's rich cultural heritage.

Chapter 3

THE GOVERNMENT OF ARIZONA

As is the case with every U.S. state, Arizona is governed at local, state, and federal levels. Counties, cities, towns, and districts (such as school districts) all have local governments. There are fifteen counties in Arizona, each of which is governed by a three-person or five-person board of supervisors. The counties with the largest populations are Maricopa, the county seat of Phoenix, and Pima, the county seat of Tucson. Towns and cities are often governed by city councils and a city manager. But some cities adopt a charter and achieve home rule. This allows them to establish their own operating structure.

Each Native American tribe in Arizona administers its own affairs through a tribal government. Tribes have their own constitutions, policies, and judicial systems.

Branches of State Government

Arizona is governed under a constitution that was approved in 1911. One provision in the original constitution nearly delayed Arizona's admission as a state. President William Taft refused to allow Arizona statehood because the state constitution allowed voters to recall

The original Arizona State Capitol Building, which opened in 1901, is now preserved as a museum telling the story of Arizona's history.

judges. The document was altered, and Arizona entered the United States. Shortly afterward, however, Arizona voters reinstated the provision allowing the recall of judges.

Arizona's state government is organized into executive, legislative, and judicial branches. The governor, who is elected to a four-year term, heads the executive branch. In the election held in 2006, Arizonans elected Governor Janet Napolitano, a Democrat, to a second term. In 2009, however, President Barack Obama appointed Napolitano to be secretary of the Department of Homeland Security.

Controversy Over Illegal Immigration

Arizona, with its Mexican border and high population of illegal immigrants, has become a new battleground in a recurring national debate over immigration. Throughout U.S. history, foreign immigration has been controversial for American citizens. Many Americans have resented the influx of immigrants, who are often viewed as poor, uneducated, and unlikely ever to assimilate into American society. During the mid-nineteenth century, nearly ten million immigrants arrived from Europe, especially from Ireland and Germany. At the end of the nineteenth century through the early twentieth century, the trend shifted to a flood of more than twenty million immigrants from Eastern and Southern Europe. With each wave of newcomers, some native-born Americans have urged the government to tighten restrictions on immigration.

Today, dealing with illegal immigration across U.S. borders is a controversial issue. About twelve million illegal immigrants live in the United States. Most of them are from Mexico and other Latin American countries. Congress has been unable to pass an immigration bill reforming the immigration system. The issue is too contentious for any compromise that would satisfy both sides: supporters of strict laws and enforcement, and those who favor approaches like amnesty and a guest worker program.

Arizonans tend to strongly support restrictions and crackdowns. Geographically, their state is at the center of the controversy. The Arizona border is the most popular crossing point for illegal immigrants. Congress has approved construction of fences along the U.S.-Mexico border, and an anti-immigration activist group called the Minutemen Project patrols the Arizona border. Arizona has also enacted some of the nation's toughest anti-immigration legislation, including a ban on social services to immigrants. Immigration reform was a key issue in the 2006 Senate campaign, with both candidates accusing the other of having supported amnesty in past votes.

A U.S. Border Patrol agent walks in front of the border fence near Nogales, Arizona. Illegal immigrants sometimes tunnel under the fences to enter the United States.

Since secretary of state is the second highest office in the executive branch, Secretary of State Jan Brewer, a Republican, stepped up to become Arizona's governor.

One of Arizona's most famous governors was Bruce Babbitt, a Democrat, who served from 1978 to 1987. As governor, Babbitt implemented a major groundwater management program, approved a highly effective health care management program, and improved the state's child welfare system. After leaving office, Babbitt ran for president in 1988—he did not win the Democratic nomination—and served as U.S. Secretary of the Interior from 1993 to 2001 under President Bill Clinton.

The state legislature—the branch of the government that makes laws—is divided into a thirty-member Senate and a sixty-member House of Representatives. The term of office is two years. Republicans have held the majority in both houses since 1993.

The Arizona State Supreme Court is the state's highest court. Lorna Lockwood, who was appointed in 1965, was the first woman in the United States to head a state supreme court. The next level in the judicial branch is the court of appeals, which has divisions in Phoenix and Tucson. Then there are superior courts and lesser courts. There is one superior court in each county.

National Representation

Arizona sends two senators to the U.S. Senate, where they serve six-year terms. In 2004, Republican John McCain was reelected to his fourth term in office. Republican Jon Kyl was reelected to his third term in 2006.

From 1912 to 1940, Arizona had only one U.S. representative in Congress because of its small population. Today, Arizona sends eight representatives—one from each of the eight districts—to the U.S. House of Representatives, where they serve two-year terms. In 2008, Arizonans elected five Democrats and three Republicans.

Two famous former representatives from Arizona are Democratic brothers Stewart Udall and Morris "Mo" Udall. Stewart spent six years in the House of Representatives and then served as U.S. Secretary of the Interior from 1961 to 1969. Mo replaced him in the House of Representatives, serving for thirty years. Mo ran for president in 1976 but did not win the Democratic nomination.

Mo Udall, speaking during his 1967 presidential campaign, was an influential and popular congressman. He was passionate about environmental issues and Native American causes.

Arizona has voted Republican in every presidential election since 1952, with one exception—Arizonans picked Bill Clinton in 1996. Two Arizonans have been nominated as the Republican candidate for president. In 1964, Senator Barry Goldwater was beaten by Lyndon Johnson. In 2008, John McCain was beaten by Barack Obama.

Two Arizonans have served on the U.S. Supreme Court. Judge William Rehnquist was appointed to the Supreme Court in 1971 and became chief justice in 1986. In 1981, Judge Sandra Day O'Connor became the first female justice to serve on the nation's highest court.

THE ECONOMY OF ARIZONA

Historically, Arizona's economy has been supported by the "Five C's": copper, cattle, cotton, citrus, and climate. Many of the first Arizona settlers were ranchers who grazed cattle on the land and miners who hoped to strike their fortunes. Small-scale mining for gold and silver eventually gave way to industrial copper mining. Arizona is the top copper-producing state in the nation. Water projects completed in the early twentieth century made agriculture possible in Arizona.

During the second half of the twentieth century, four of the "Five C's" were overshadowed economically by the manufacturing and service sectors. Arizona's agreeable climate, however, continues to attract tourists and new residents. People are drawn by the endless sunny days, warm winter temperatures, and year-round outdoor recreational opportunities. Arizona's dry air and high-altitude terrain also create perfect conditions for astronomical observation. Three observatories in southern Arizona have put Tucson at the center of astronomical research. In 1930, an astronomer working at the Lowell Observatory near Flagstaff discovered Pluto.

Like the U.S. economy in general, Arizona has been impacted by the recession that began in 2007. The state has been severely affected because of the drop in real estate prices and homebuilding. Throughout 2008, wages and the value of assets like stockholdings decreased, and unemployment rates increased. Home prices fell, and Phoenix became one of the U.S. cities hardest hit by rising rates of foreclosure.

Agriculture

Livestock and crops each make up about half of Arizona's agricultural output. Raising beef cattle, calves, and dairy cows generates the most revenue of any agricultural sector. Other livestock raised in Arizona include sheep and hogs.

Arizona produces 20 percent of the nation's lettuce, the state's biggest crop. Cotton became an important crop during World War I. In Arizona's climate, cotton farmers can harvest

Arizona cotton crops produce the highest yield per acre of any U.S. state. Most of Arizona's cotton is exported overseas.

crops three times a year. Today, cotton is Arizona's second most valuable crop. Other crops include wheat, vegetables like cauliflower and broccoli, melons, citrus fruit, potatoes, and sweet potatoes.

Mining and Manufacturing

The days of mining boomtowns are long gone, but copper mining still contributes to the state's economy. Gold, silver, gravel, coal, and

The Water Issue

The scarcity of water has threatened human survival in Arizona for as long as people have inhabited the area.

Beginning in the seventh century, the Hohokam people of central Arizona began building an elaborate canal system to irrigate crops. They constructed hundreds—perhaps even thousands—of miles of sophisticated canals connected to the Salt and Gila rivers. Crops, which included corn, beans, squash, grains, and cotton, were planted between the canals and near natural water sources. The Hohokam also hunted the animals that were attracted by the crops.

In 1867, adventurer and Confederate army deserter Jack Swilling encountered the Hohokam ruins. Swilling took a look at the Hohokam ruins and realized that it was possible for people to practice agriculture in the harsh desert. Swilling proceeded to organize the Swilling Irrigation and Canal Company and began reclaiming the Hohokam cropland. Eventually, the town that sprang up in the area was called Phoenix, after the mythological bird, symbolizing the emergence of new life from ancient ruins.

Today, massive dams and the completion of the Central Arizona Project (CAP), which diverts water from the Colorado River, provide reliable sources of water and hydroelectric power. These projects have significantly altered Arizona's natural geography.

With water a valuable resource, the matter of water rights has proven to be a controversial one over the years. The dispute between Arizona and California over Colorado River water rights has repeatedly gone before the Supreme Court.

Potential water shortages remain an issue in the Southwest. Drought, climate change, and continued population growth could someday strain the water supply and ravage natural habitats.

molybdenum are also mined in Arizona. Uranium has been found on Navajo and Hopi reservations.

Arizona's manufacturing sector expanded during and after World War II, when the government built military facilities in the state. Today, leading manufactured products include computer and electronic equipment, such as semiconductors. The manufacture of transportation equipment is also a major industry. Arizona factories produce aerospace vehicles, turbine engines, helicopters, and guided missiles.

Trucks, a power shovel, and other equipment operate in a copper mine near Tucson. Arizona is the leading copper producer in the United States.

Service Sector

The service sector accounts for the largest segment of Arizona's economy. The service sector includes financial institutions (such as real estate and insurance businesses), retail, hospitality and leisure (such as hotels and restaurants), professional services (such as legal firms), and government institutions (such as schools and military facilities). The state government employs more Arizonans than any other entity. Wal-Mart is the state's biggest private employer. Construction is also an important economic sector in Arizona.

Tourism is highly profitable for the service sector, contributing about $12 billion annually to the state's economy. Tourists spend money on hotels, transportation, amenities, and souvenirs ranging from cactus key chains to folk art. They spend time on golf courses, at resorts, in casinos, near ancient ruins, at rodeos, and on guest ranches. They flock to the Grand Canyon and other parks and monuments. Visitors can even see the London Bridge—it was transported from England to Arizona in the 1960s and reopened near Lake Havasu City in 1971.

Chapter 5

PEOPLE FROM ARIZONA:
PAST AND PRESENT

Arizona has a rich past, which helped cultivate a variety of talented people. From great writers to leaders, musicians, and politicians, Arizona has been home to more than a few notable names.

Edward Abbey (1927–1989) Abbey, who lived in Oracle, was a writer who championed the preservation of the wilderness. He is known for his vivid and impassioned descriptions of the American West and his opposition to the development and mismanagement of the land. His best-known books are *Desert Solitaire*, an account based on his stint as a park ranger, and the novel *The Monkey Wrench Gang*.

Cesar Chavez (1927–1993) Chavez, born in Yuma, was a labor organizer who attracted international attention to the hardships of farm workers. In 1962, he founded the union that later became the United Farm Workers. Three years later, his union participated in a strike against grape growers, and Chavez organized a grape boycott. As a result, most of the grape growers signed contracts with the union in 1969.

Cesar Chavez's family lost their farm during the Great Depression. They traveled around for the next ten years looking for work in the fields.

Cochise (1815–1874)

Cochise was a chief among the Chiricahua Apache who led an uprising against American settlers. Tensions arose between the Apache and white settlers in 1861 when Cochise was falsely accused of kidnapping a rancher's son. For the next ten years, he and his men led raids against troops, settlers, and traders. Cochise surrendered in 1872 and retreated to a newly established reservation.

Geronimo (1829–1909)

Geronimo was an Apache leader renowned for his ferocity and fearlessness. He led the Chiricahau after Cochise's death, and his men resumed attacks against white settlers in 1874 after the Apache were forced onto an inhospitable reservation. Geronimo surrendered in 1886.

Zane Grey (1872–1939) Grey was the prolific and best-selling author credited with developing the Western as a literary form. Born in Ohio, Grey moved to California as a young man and spent time every year in his Arizona hunting lodge. He wrote more than ninety books, including *Riders of the Purple Sage.*

Eusebio Kino (1645–1711) The Italian-born Jesuit priest Eusebio Kino established twenty-two missions in New Spain, including the first three in present-day Arizona. He brought new agricultural practices to Native Americans and opposed their forced labor in silver mines. Kino was also an accomplished mapmaker, astronomer, and intrepid explorer who proved that Baja California was a peninsula, rather than an island.

After his surrender, Geronimo was sent to a prison in Florida and eventually settled in Oklahoma as a prisoner of war.

Percival Lowell (1855–1916) The Boston-born astronomer Percival Lowell founded the Lowell Observatory in Flagstaff in 1894. He believed, incorrectly, that Mars was inhabited. He theorized more accurately about Pluto's existence and position in space. The Lowell Observatory is now a national landmark.

Phil Mickelson (1970–) Born in San Diego, Mickelson grew up in California and Arizona, and attended the University

Presidential Dreams

Two Arizona politicians, Barry Goldwater and John McCain, ran for president, though their presidential bids occurred nearly fifty years apart. Both men ran on the Republican ticket. Neither won the election.

Barry Goldwater (1909–1998) was born in Phoenix just three years before Arizona became a U.S. state. He entered local politics in Phoenix in 1949 after serving in the Air Force during World War II. In 1952, he was elected U.S. senator from Arizona. During the 1960s, Goldwater emerged as the voice of a new American conservative movement. He opposed excessive government spending, especially on social programs, and supported a strong military. Goldwater ran as the Republican nominee for president in 1964, but the public saw his political viewpoints as extremist. He lost badly to Lyndon B. Johnson, receiving only 38.8 percent of the vote. Nonetheless, Goldwater later returned to the Senate for three more terms. His conservative views eventually became more widely accepted, and many policies of President Ronald Reagan reflected Goldwater's ideology.

John McCain, born in 1936, came from a family with a long history of military service. He graduated from the U.S. Naval Academy in 1958 and served as a Navy pilot during the Vietnam War. Captured by the North Vietnamese in 1967, he was held as a prisoner of war until 1973. McCain retired from the Navy and moved to Arizona in 1981. He was elected U.S. representative in 1982. When Goldwater retired from the U.S. Senate in 1985, McCain successfully ran for his seat. In 1999, McCain launched a presidential bid. He failed to receive the Republican nomination, but his campaign gained him a national following. In 2008, McCain again ran for president, this time achieving the Republican nomination. The presidential race was dominated by the issue of the deteriorating economy. Democratic candidate Barack Obama received 53 percent of the vote, defeating McCain, who received 46 percent. After the election, McCain returned to serve in the Senate.

of Arizona. "Lefty" Mickelson has been one of the most successful golfers in the Professional Golfers' Association (PGA) since his professional debut in 1992. His thirty-five career wins—including the Masters in 2004 and 2006, and the PGA championship in 2005—are second best among active golfers.

Charles Mingus (1922–1979) The innovative jazz musician and composer Charles Mingus was born in Nogales. He was a virtuoso bass player and bandleader who could inspire his musicians to reach new heights of creativity. Mingus recorded more than a hundred albums, sometimes collaborating with other jazz greats like Louis Armstrong and Charlie Parker.

Sandra Day O'Connor (1930–) O'Connor served as an assistant attorney general in Arizona from 1965 to 1969. She was a state senator from 1969 to 1974, becoming the first female majority leader in U.S. history in 1972. She was elected superior court judge in 1975 and was raised to the Arizona Court of Appeals in 1979. In 1981, O'Connor became

Before becoming a Supreme Court Justice, Sandra Day O'Connor supported the elimination of discrimination against women.

the first woman appointed to the U.S. Supreme Court, serving until 2006. Though conservative, she sometimes sided with the liberal minority.

John Wesley Powell (1834–1902) In 1869, Powell led the first expedition down the Colorado River through the Grand Canyon, despite having lost an arm at the Civil War Battle of Shiloh. Throughout the 1870s, Powell explored the Colorado Plateau. In 1880, he became director of the U.S. Geological Survey and advocated conservation of the natural resources of the West. He was also an anthropologist who studied Native American language and customs.

William Rehnquist (1924–2005) Born in Wisconsin, Rehnquist moved to Phoenix after serving in World War II and practiced law there for sixteen years. He served as the assistant attorney general from 1969 to 1971 in President Richard Nixon's administration. In 1971, Nixon nominated him justice of the Supreme Court. President Ronald Reagan nominated Rehnquist chief justice in 1986. Rehnquist was a strong conservative voice on the Supreme Court.

Leslie Marmon Silko (1948–) Tucson resident Leslie Marmon Silko is the acclaimed author of *Ceremony* and other novels that have established her as a powerful voice in Native American literature. Her work has been shaped by her growing up in New Mexico of mixed Laguna Pueblo, Mexican, and white descent. She was awarded a MacArthur Foundation Fellowship in 1981.

Timeline

1539	Marcos de Niza is the first European to enter what is present-day Arizona.
1680	Spaniards are driven from the Southwest by the Pueblo Revolt.
1752	Tubac is founded.
1821	Mexico gains independence and takes possession of present-day Arizona.
1848	Mexican territory is ceded to the United States under the Treaty of Guadalupe Hidalgo.
1854	The United States signs the Gadsden Purchase with Mexico.
1863	The Territory of Arizona is established.
1864	Kit Carson defeats the Navajo and sends the people on the "Long Walk."
1869	John Wesley Powell leads the first expedition through the Grand Canyon.
1881	The famous gunfight occurs at O.K. Corral.
1886	Geronimo surrenders, ending the Indian Wars.
1911	Theodore Roosevelt Dam is completed.
1912	Arizona becomes the forty-eighth state.
1919	Grand Canyon National Park is founded.
1936	Hoover Dam is completed.
1991	Central Arizona Project (CAP) is completed.
2002	The worst wildfire in state history ravages more than 450,000 acres (182,108 hectares) of land in central Arizona.
2007	The Hualapai tribe opens the glass-floored Grand Canyon Skywalk extending 70 feet (21 m) past the canyon's edge.
2008	Senator John McCain runs for U.S. president as the Republican nominee.
2009	Governor Janet Napolitano is named Secretary of Homeland Security.

State motto	*Ditat Deus* ("God enriches.")
State capital	Phoenix
State song	"Arizona"
State flower	Saguaro blossom
State bird	Cactus wren
State tree	Palo Verde
Statehood date and number	February 14, 1912; forty-eighth state
State nickname	Grand Canyon State
Total area and U.S. rank	114,007 square miles (295,278 sq km); sixth-largest state
Population	6,166,318
Highest elevation	Humphrey's Peak, at 12,633 feet (3,851 m)
Lowest elevation	Colorado River, at 75 feet (21 m)
Major rivers	Colorado River, Gila River, Salt River, San Pedro River, Little Colorado River

State Flag

State Seal

Major lakes	Lake Mead, Theodore Roosevelt Lake, San Carlos Lake, Lake Havasu, Lake Powell, Lake Mojave, Apache Lake
Hottest recorded temperature	128°F (53°C) in Lake Havasu City, on June 29, 1994
Coldest recorded temperature	-40°F (-4°C) at Hawley Lake, on January 7, 1971
Origin of state name	May be derived from a place-name meaning "small spring," or it could be the Basque word for "the good oak tree"
Chief agricultural products	Cattle, hogs, sheep, hay, cotton, wheat, vegetables, fruit, potatoes, sweet potatoes
Major industries	Computer and electronic equipment, transportation equipment, chemicals

State Bird

State Flower

GLOSSARY

butte An isolated mountain or hill with sloping sides and a flat top that rises abruptly above the surrounding area.

canal An artificial waterway or artificially improved river used for irrigation, shipping, or transportation.

canyon A long, deep, narrow valley with steep cliff walls, often formed by running water and having a river or stream at the bottom.

constitution The system of fundamental laws and principles that prescribes the nature, functions, and limits of a government or other institution.

drought A long period of abnormally low rainfall, especially one that adversely affects growing or living conditions.

ecosystem A system formed by a community of organisms and their interactions with their physical environment.

immigrant A person who enters and establishes residence in a country or region in which he or she is not a native.

mesa An isolated land formation, larger in area than a butte, with steep walls and a flat top.

missionary A person sent out, often to a foreign country, to convert others to a particular religion or other doctrine.

petroglyph A rock carving or line drawing, especially one made by prehistoric people.

plateau An area of relatively flat, elevated ground.

prospector A person who explores a region for mineral deposits or precious metals.

recession A decline in business activity in an economy lasting for at least a few months.

sagebrush A small aromatic shrub with silver-green wedge-shaped leaves and clusters of yellow flowers that grows in semiarid regions of the American West.

saguaro cactus A very large branched cactus of the Sonoran Desert that bears white flowers with yellow centers and a red edible fruit.

Arizona Historical Society

Arizona History Museum

949 East 2nd Street

Tucson, AZ 85719

(520) 628-5774

Web site: http://www.arizonahistoricalsociety.org/museums/#tuc

The Arizona History Museum explores the state's history from Spanish colonial times through the territorial eras. It also exhibits the history of Arizona's mining and transportation industries.

Arizona State Library, Archives and Public Records

1700 West Washington, Suite 200

Phoenix, AZ 85007

(602) 926-4035

Web site: http://www.azlibrary.gov

This Arizona institution provides citizens with access to unique historical and contemporary resources.

Arizona State Museum

University of Arizona

1013 East University Boulevard

P.O. Box 210026

Tucson, AZ 85721-0026

(520) 621-6302

Web site: http://www.statemuseum.arizona.edu

Sponsored by the University of Arizona, the Arizona State Museum was established in 1893 and is the oldest and largest anthropology museum in the Southwest.

Grand Canyon National Park

Center Loop Road

Grand Canyon National Park, AZ 86001

(928) 638-7888

Web site: http://www.nps.gov/grca

Information about the Grand Canyon National Park can be found on its Web site.

Heard Museum

2301 North Central Avenue

Phoenix, AZ 85004

(602) 252-8840

Web site: http://www.heard.org

This museum is world-famous for its collection of Native American crafts and fine art.

Navajo Nation

The Navajo Nation

P.O. Box 9000

Window Rock, AZ 86515

(928) 871-6000

Web site: http://www.navajo.org

This official Web site of the Navajo Nation provides news, events, history, and more on the Navajo.

Web Sites

Due to the changing nature of Internet links, Rosen Publishing has developed an online list of Web sites related to the subject of this book. This site is updated regularly. Please use this link to access this list:

http://www.rosenlinks.com/uspp/azpp

FOR FURTHER READING

Croy, Anita. *Ancient Pueblo: Archaeology Unlocks the Secrets of America's Past*. Washington, DC: National Geographic, 2007.

Ghose, Aruna, ed. *Arizona and the Grand Canyon*. New York, NY: DK Publishing, Inc., 2005.

Graf, Mike. *Grand Canyon: The Tail of the Scorpion*. Golden, CO: Fulcrum Publishing, 2006.

Hayes, Allan and Carol. *The Desert Southwest: Four Thousand Years of Life and Art*. Berkeley, CA: Ten Speed Press, 2006.

Holm, Tom. *Code Talkers and Warriors: Native Americans and World War II*. New York, NY: Chelsea House, 2007.

Iverson, Peter. *The Navajo*. Philadelphia, PA: Chelsea House Publishers, 2005.

Jameson, W. C. *Buried Treasures of the American Southwest*. Little Rock, AK: August House, 2006.

Kallen, Stuart A. *The Grand Canyon*. San Diego, CA: Kidhaven Press, 2003.

Landau, Elaine. *Wyatt Earp: Wild West Lawman*. Berkeley Heights, NJ: Enslow Publishers, 2004.

Logan, Michael. *Desert Cities: The Environmental History of Phoenix and Tucson*. Pittsburgh, PA: University of Pittsburgh Press, 2006.

McDaniel, Melissa, and Wendy Mead. *Arizona*. Tarrytown, NY: Marshall Cavendish Benchmark, 2009.

Melody, Michael E. *The Apache*. Philadelphia, PA: Chelsea House Publishers, 2006.

Souza, Dorothy M. *John Wesley Powell*. New York, NY: Franklin Watts, 2004.

Utley, Robert M., ed. *The Story of the West: A History of the American West and Its People*. New York, NY: DK Publishing, Inc., 2003.

Wiewandt, Thomas, and Maureen Wilks. *The Southwest—Inside Out: An Illustrated Guide to the Land and Its History*. 2nd ed. Tucson, AZ: Wild Horizons Publishing, 2004.

Young, Jeff C. *Cesar Chavez*. Greensboro, NC: Morgan Reynolds Publishing, 2007.

Andrews, John P., and Todd W. Bostwick. "Desert Farmers at the River's Edge: The Hohokam and Pueblo Grande." Phoenix.gov. Retrieved March 25, 2009 (http://phoenix.gov/PUEBLO/dfharves.html).

Cheek, Lawrence W. *Compass American Guides: Arizona*. New York, NY: Fodors LLC, 2004.

Desert USA. "Cochise, Geronimo, and Mangas Coloradas." Retrieved March 25, 2009 (http://www.desertusa.com/magfeb98/feb_pap/du_apache.html).

McClory, Toni. "Arizona Local Government Factsheet." Glendale Community College of Arizona. Retrieved March 1, 2009 (http://web.gccaz.edu/~tmcclory/Factsheets/Factsheet_AZlocal.pdf).

Metz, Leon Claire. *The Shooters: A Gallery of Notorious Gunmen from the American West*. New York, NY: Berkley Books, 1996.

Newton, Jim. "James Q. Wilson: The Power of His Written Word." *Los Angeles Times*, June 3, 2007. Retrieved March 25, 2009 (http://www.latimes.com/news/opinion/la-op-newton3jun03,0,2931003,full.story).

Samson, Karl. *Frommer's Arizona*. Hoboken, NJ: Wiley Publishing, Inc., 2008.

SHG Resources. "Guide to Arizona History." Retrieved March 1, 2009 (http://www.shgresources.com/az/history).

Vest, Marshall J. "Economic Outlook for 2009–2010: Riding Out the Storm." University of Arizona, December 1, 2008. Retrieved March 1, 2009 (http://ebr.eller.arizona.edu/AZEconomy).

Weir, Bill. *Moon Handbooks Arizona*. Emeryville, CA: Avalon Travel Publishing, 2005.

INDEX

About the Author

Corona Brezina has written more than a dozen titles for Rosen Publishing. Several of her previous books have also focused on American history and current events, including *Great Historic Speeches: Sojourner Truth: Ain't I a Woman* and *Extreme Environmental Threats: Disappearing Forests*. She lives in Chicago.

Photo Credits

Cover (top left) Courtesy Arizona Historical Society, Tuscon; cover (top right) © www.istockphoto.com/constantgardener; cover (bottom), pp. 8, 13, 31 Shutterstock.com; pp. 3, 7, 15, 22, 23, 28, 33, 39, 41 Wikimedia Commons; p. 4 (top) © GeoAtlas; p. 10 Courtesy Arizona Game and Fish Department; p. 12 Hulton Archive/Getty Images; p. 16 Transcendental Graphics/Hulton Archive/Getty Images; p. 19 Stock Montage/Hulton Archive/Getty Images; p. 21 Keystone/Hulton Archive/Getty Images; p. 25 © AP Images; p. 27 Arnold Sachs/Hulton Archive/Getty Images; p. 29 © www.istockphoto.com/Bruce Bean; p. 34 Geoff Hansen/Getty Images; p. 35 Library of Congress Prints and Photographs Division; p. 37 Brendan Smialowski/Getty Images; p. 40 (left) Courtesy of Robesus, Inc.

Designer: Les Kanturek; Editor: Nicholas Croce;
Photo Researcher: Cindy Reiman